Dear Scott,
Happy Fathers Day
2006

Love,
Mom & Dad

A Father's Covenant

Stephen Gabriel

A Father's Covenant

173 Promises

for Consideration

and Reflection

HarperSanFrancisco
An Imprint of HarperCollins*Publishers*

HarperCollins Web Site: http://www.harpercollins.com
HarperCollins®, ≜®, and HarperSanFrancisco™ are trademarks of HarperCollins Publishers Inc.

FIRST EDITION

ISBN 0-06-063160-0 (pbk.)

96 97 98 99 00 ❖HAD 10 9 8 7 6 5 4 3 2 1

To my parents,
who gave me my
first lessons
in love

Contents

Preface   ix

Promises to My Wife

    Our Romance 3

    Our Family 21

Promises to My Children

    On Religion 35

    On Discipline 43

    On Family Living 55

Promises to Myself

    My Spiritual Life 75

    My Family Life 87

    My Friends and Community 101

Preface

This little book is meant to be a kind of compass for fathers navigating the tricky waters of fatherhood. The proposed promises embody a spirit of service and leadership grounded in Christian virtues.

First come the promises to your wife. These promises lay the groundwork for a happy marriage—the best gift anyone could give a child. The promises to children are based on a relationship founded on religious faith, implemented through a discipline of love in a setting of intimate family life. The promises made to oneself define areas of struggle that, if pursued with perseverance, will make us better fathers.

The specifics of any one promise may or may not be appropriate for a given reader. However, the essence of the promise should be. For example, whether you promise to work an eight-hour, nine-hour, or ten-hour day as a rule is not as important as the commitment to being available to your wife and family a sufficient number of hours per day. The point is, a family needs a father's presence!

This book will be a success if it inspires you to make and struggle to keep one promise you otherwise would not have made, bringing you closer to God, your wife, and your children. Indeed, you will have become a better father just for having made the promise.

A Father's Covenant

Part 1

Promises to
MY WIFE

Chapter One

To My Wife:
Our Romance

— 1 —

I will continue
to court you.

— 2 —

I will find ways to keep
the embers of our
romance glowing.

— 3 —

I will remind you often why
I married you and assure you
that I'd do it again.

I will call you
during the day
and tell you that
I love you.

— 5 —

I will occasionally bring
flowers to you for no
apparent reason.

— 6 —

I will cherish the intimacy
that is unique to us.

— 7 —

I will accept some responsibility
for our children's undesirable
traits and habits.

— 8 —

I will take you
away from the kids
(overnight) at least
once a year.

— 9 —

I will ask you to
walk around the
neighborhood with me
on pleasant
summer evenings.

I will take

you out on an

inexpensive date

regularly.

— 11 —

I will not disdain
Valentine's Day.

— 12 —

I will try to listen
attentively even when
I don't really
feel like it.

— 13 —

I will listen to the
details of your day.

— 14 —

I will give you
focused attention.

— 15 —

I will share my thoughts
and concerns with you.

— 16 —

I will try to learn to
love your shortcomings
while I struggle to
overcome my own.

I will develop
a foolproof
method of
remembering your
birthday and
our wedding
anniversary.

— 18 —

I will ask your opinion
when I am concocting
my latest project.

— 19 —

I will remind myself that
you really are my better half.

— 20 —

I will try to put down what
I am doing and go to bed
when you want to.

— 21 —

I will not
go to bed angry.

— 22 —

I will compliment you
on your cooking.

— 23 —

I will hope to have cause
to compliment.

I will surprise
you with a meal
from time to time,
and ignore the
skeptical looks from
the kids.

~ 25 ~

I will not get fat
(too fat).

~ 26 ~

I will remind myself
that, like all worthwhile
endeavors, marriage
takes effort.

~ 27 ~

I will not fear exposing
my heart to you.

— 28 —

I will try not to be
the cross you are called
to bear daily, but the
friend that helps you
bear the crosses that
come your way.

— 29 —

I will not take
advantage of those
vulnerabilities that your
love exposes to me.

I will regard
our marriage as
a holy alliance
for our sanctification
and that of our
children.

— 31 —

I will remember that
our marriage is the
foundation upon which
our children will build
their marriages.

— 32 —

I will teach our
children by my example
to hold you in the
highest esteem.

Chapter Two

To My Wife: Our Family

— 33 —

I will work an
eight-hour day.

— 34 —

I will travel away from
home with my work as
little as possible.

— 35 —

I will struggle to be
cheerful at home in spite
of financial and
work-related concerns.

— 36 —

I will not
bring my work
home with me.

~ 37 ~

I will insist on
having dinner together
as a family.

~ 38 ~

I will pray
for you daily.

~ 39 ~

I will help
with the housework.

~ 40 ~

I will change
dirty diapers.

~ 41 ~

I will help with the
kids' homework.

~ 42 ~

I will put my dirty
clothes in the hamper.

I will consult
with you when
practical before
punishing a child.

— 44 —

I will clean out
the lint trap in the
clothes dryer without
complaining to you that
you never do.

— 45 —

I will try to plan,
encourage, and enjoy
family outings.

— 46 —

I will remember that you and
I are our children's primary
educators. Every facet of
their education is our
responsibility.

— 47 —

I will encourage you to
pursue "extracurricular"
activities, and support you
by being available to
watch the kids.

I will make sure
that the kids are
used to seeing
me display my
affection for you.

― 49 ―

I will try not to make
too much noise while
watching evening football
games after you've
gone to bed.

― 50 ―

I will acknowledge that
I cannot fulfill the
demands of our marriage
alone. I will pray for
the grace to succeed as
a husband and father.

I promise my wife . . .

_____

_____

_____

_____

_____

_____

_____

_____

_____

_____

_____

_____

_____

. . . and I will persevere in my effort, knowing that
at times I will fail even as I begin again and again.

Part 2

Promises to MY CHILDREN

Chapter Three

To My Children: On Religion

— 51 —

I will make sure you know
that I pray and that Jesus Christ
is the model for my life.

— 52 —

I will pray for you daily.

— 53 —

I will pray specifically
for your salvation.

I will teach you
that you are
important enough
for Jesus to have
suffered on the cross
for you alone.

— 55 —

I will talk to you
about God.

— 56 —

I will teach you
that I am a child
in the eyes of God.

— 57 —

I will try not to get in
the way if you receive a special
calling from God.

— 58 —

I will communicate,
by word and deed,
my high moral
expectations of you.

— 59 —

I will forgive you.

— 60 —

I will ask for your
forgiveness.

I will teach you
that your faith
is your most
precious
possession.

— 62 —

I will insist that
you dress well for
church on Sunday.

— 63 —

I will teach you not to
fear poverty because, as a
Christian, you may be
served well by poverty.

Chapter Four

To My Children: On Discipline

∽ 64 ∽

I will demand
respect from you.

∽ 65 ∽

I will demand that you
show your mother
great respect.

∽ 66 ∽

I will always
trust you.

I will explain
to you that I always
trust your integrity;
I don't always trust
your judgment.

~ 68 ~

I will not give you much
spending money.

~ 69 ~

I will say no often.

~ 70 ~

I will try to explain
why I say no.

— 71 —

I will allow
you to watch
very little TV.

— 72 —

I will make sure
that you have specific
chores and
responsibilities
at home.

I will not expect
you to make A's in
school. I will
expect you to
do your best.

— 74 —

I will presume the
good intentions of my
daughters' dates.

— 75 —

I will instruct my daughters
about the effects of testosterone
in teenage boys.

— 76 —

I will teach my sons that
chastity is a masculine word.

— 77 —

I will teach you
that there are consequences
to your behavior.

— 78 —

I will teach you
that true freedom is not
being free to do whatever
you want but being free
to choose the good.

I will pray for
the wisdom to
know when and
how to let go
of you as you grow
and mature.

— 80 —

I will respect your
legitimate freedom.

— 81 —

I will teach you that
with freedom comes
responsibility.

— 82 —

I will correct
you without
demeaning you.

— 83 —

I will pray especially
for the child who is
annoying me the most.

— 84 —

I will make you a
stranger to instant
gratification.

Chapter Five

To My Children: On Family Living

— 85 —

I will wrestle
with you on the
living room floor.

— 86 —

I will hug you daily.

— 87 —

I will even hug my
teenagers often.

I will teach you
that there is
objective truth.

~ 89 ~

I will learn to play sports
that you like to play.

~ 90 ~

I will read to you when
you are little.

~ 91 ~

I will go to Little League
baseball games and try to
look interested.

— 92 —

I will play
Chutes and Ladders
with enthusiasm.

— 93 —

I will put my money
into your primary and
secondary education first
and college second.

I will tuck
you into bed
at night.

— 95 —

I will give my daughters
the attention and affection
they need, teaching them
that pure love is the
only real love.

— 96 —

I will make sure you know
that I am madly in love
with your mother.

— 97 —

I will teach you that some
things are subject to opinion
and some things are not.

— 98 —

I will not compare you
with one another.

— 99 —

I will meet the parents
of your friends.

I will love you
unconditionally.

~ 101 ~

I will not impose
career expectations
on you.

~ 102 ~

I will teach you that it is
all right to be different.

~ 103 ~

I will teach you
that in many matters
you must be different.

— 104 —

I will try to be
patient with you.

— 105 —

I will seek to be involved
in your life without
smothering you.

— 106 —

I will put the newspaper
down when you want
to talk to me.

I will send you to a
school that will
reinforce the values
that I want you
to learn.

~ 108 ~

I will attend
school functions.

~ 109 ~

I will make sure that
I know and approve of
your teachers and the
spirit of your school.

~ 110 ~

I will pursue hobbies
that can involve you.

— 111 —

I will teach you to give a
firm handshake and look the
recipient in the eye.

— 112 —

I will take you to help
at a soup kitchen from
time to time.

— 113 —

I will talk to you
about my childhood.

I will challenge my
teenage sons to a
game of one—on—one
basketball, knowing
that they will relish
the slaughter after
years of being
trounced by me.

— 115 —

I will try not to be
unnecessarily critical
of your friends.

— 116 —

I will introduce
you to classical music.

I promise my children . . .

_____

_____

_____

_____

_____

_____

_____

_____

_____

_____

. . . and I will pray that my mistakes will be small
and that my love for you will dissipate the faults
that cloud my vision as a father.

Part 3

Promises to
MYSELF

Chapter Six

To Myself:
My Spiritual Life

~ 117 ~

I will examine my
conscience daily.

~ 118 ~

I will identify a particular
fault or vice that I have
and make a serious effort to
eradicate it.

~ 119 ~

I will make a plan
to grow spiritually.

I will be firm
in my belief
that my faith
is the true faith
and worth
dying for.

— 121 —

I will reflect on
the cross as a symbol of
my faith and all that it
demands of a disciple
of Christ.

— 122 —

I will show that
I am tolerant of people
of other faiths.

— 123 —

I will seek God's
help regularly.

— 124 —

I will be generous
in supporting
the Church.

— 125 —

I will pray daily.

I will try to
view the events
of my life within
the context of
my spiritual
journey to
heaven.

— 127 —

I will not criticize
the clergy.

— 128 —

I will seek a situation
where such criticism
is not necessary.

— 129 —

If I must correct the
clergy, I will do so
with charity.

— 130 —

I will entrust my
family to God's
Providence.

— 131 —

I will believe
in miracles.

— 132 —

I will endeavor
to make my work
a prayer.

I will not be
afraid to
begin again.

— 134 —

I will remember
that I will not be given
a burden too heavy
for me to bear.

— 135 —

I will consider
how well off
I really am.

— 136 —

I will consider
my life a unity of
God, family, work,
and friendship.

— 137 —

I will remember
that God will not be
outdone in generosity.

Chapter Seven

To Myself: My Family Life

— 138 —

I will try
to remember that
my role is to serve.

— 139 —

I will foster friendships
with families who
will reinforce the values
I want for my family.

I will watch
TV very little.

— 141 —

I will make sure
the shows I watch
on TV reflect the
values I want my
family to live by.

— 142 —

I will put others first.

— 143 —

I will practice
what I preach.

— 144 —

I will try to foster extended
family relationships and
teach my children what
a treasure family is—
grandparents, aunts,
uncles, cousins . . . .

— 145 —

I will try to remember that
my words and actions
will influence people
long after I die.

— 146 —

I will remember
that my work
is a means to an
end — not the
end itself.

~ 147 ~

I will pick a job around
the house that I hate to do
and do it secretly.

~ 148 ~

I will apologize
frequently.

~ 149 ~

I will bite my
tongue regularly.

— 150 —

I will try to remember
that my children have been
given to me on loan.

— 151 —

I will remind myself
that actions speak louder
than words. My kids will
remember what I do more
than what I say.

I will pray
for the virtues:
wisdom, fortitude,
patience.

‒ 153 ‒

I will try to make
time to read.

‒ 154 ‒

I will call
my parents on a
regular basis.

— 155 —

I will try to purge
our home of any trace
of a critical spirit while
being uncompromising
in matters of faith
and morals.

— 156 —

I will not be afraid
to struggle.

I will try to foster
family pride and
loyalty without being
obnoxious about it.

Chapter Eight

To Myself:
My Friends and
Community

— 158 —

I will work hard.

— 159 —

I will be generous
with my time.

— 160 —

I will work like
everything depends on
me and pray like
everything depends
on God.

I will try

not to be

mean to cats.

~ 162 ~

I will show a respect
for rightful authority.

~ 163 ~

I will vote.

~ 164 ~

I will be a good
friend to my friends.

— 165 —

I will be honest
in paying my taxes.

— 166 —

I will call one friend
per week.

— 167 —

I will seek to give
back more than
I receive, knowing
that I never can.

I will not take myself too seriously.

— 169 —

I will shovel my
neighbor's sidewalk
when I know he needs
the help.

— 170 —

I will not gossip.

— 171 —

I will not make
comfort a central
goal of my life.

I will reflect on my
life and my lifestyle and
then consider the words of
Christ: "If anyone wishes to
come after me, let him deny
himself, take up his cross
daily and follow me."
(Luke 9:23)

I will not minimize
the importance
of little things in my
relationship with
God, my family,
and friends.

I promise myself . . .

_____

_____

_____

_____

_____

_____

_____

_____

_____

_____

. . . and I will pray for the grace and the
virtues that will enable me to submit my
will to that of my Father, God.

To Myself: My Friends and Community